Legacies & Encounters

POEMS 1966–1971

KAREN GERSHON

LONDON

VICTOR GOLLANCZ LTD

1972

B|

ISBN 0 575 01454 7

PRINTED IN GREAT BRITAIN
BY EBENEZER BAYLIS & SON LIMITED
THE TRINITY PRESS, WORCESTER, AND LONDON

LEGACIES & ENCOUNTERS

POEMS 1966–1971

Poetry by Karen Gershon:

The Relentless Year (New Poets 1959, Eyre & Spottiswoode, 1960)

Selected Poems (Victor Gollancz Ltd., 1966)

Non-fiction:

We Came as Children (a collective autobiography of refugees, 1966)

Postscript (a collective account of the lives of Jews in West Germany since the Second World War, 1969)

Contents

Acknowledgements

Acknowledgements are due to:

The Critical Quarterly

The London Magazine

Encounter

The New York Times, U.S.A.

The Jerusalem Post, Israel

The 'Jerusalem Poems' have been published, with a Hebrew translation by Rahel Chalfi, by Ecked, Tel Aviv.

LEGACIES & ENCOUNTERS

POEMS 1966–1971

MONOLOGUES

I
Children are Windfalls

Children who might have been mine
from choice or by chance
wait till I am alone
to come out and prance
on my mind's stage
as if I were a barren peasant
beset with age

All children are windfalls
sometimes these others
are suddenly present
as sounds are in bells
in their sisters and brothers

II
Mothers Waiting

Mothers waiting for school to be out
are patient and content
but how much we resent
our children when we are faced with them

In anticipation proud
in reality we feel
a mixture of guilt for the dream
and shame at the facts they reveal

III
A Mother Said

I shall throw her out of the nest
now that she is old enough
to manage on her own
and make more room for the rest

She is making room for herself
for seventeen years she has been
a beehive for this queen

IV
A Signpost

Not to please her but to provide
something she will remember later
I have planned this day for my daughter
to serve as her guide
down this path of my mind
when I have left her behind

V
Stella's Eyes

My daughter grieves over inadequate eyes
they are an example of
love being not enough
nobody else can see what she can see

All appearances are a disguise
we all look at the world alone
she wears her body wrapped about
her vulnerability
so that it is as hard to look in
as it is for her to look out

VI

Stella's Imperfections

Perfection makes my daughter self-contained
when I admire her I make no claim
imperfections which we share
make me feel related to her
I discover them with love
and am ashamed
because however much I disapprove
I cannot wish her to be free of them

VII

Christopher's Grief

Grief makes my growing children withdraw from
tentative outposts and turn back to me
sad that only life's hostility
can prolong my usefulness to them

A sudden need for being comforted
contradicts my son's age
briefly he has reverted to the stage
of having faith in me and being led

VIII

Looking after Naomi

Why, when I do so much for her all day long,
do I resent some minor demand she makes?
This pressure on each moment till it breaks,
is it not spring?

When she pours her existence into the mould of my day,
what a vessel she fashions!
What value would I have left to lock away
if she did not count me among her possessions?

IX
Naomi Praised
I need to hear my children praised
they are the pyramids I build
and like a slave I only see
immediate concerns to me

Spectators view the total child
the shape revealed leaves me amazed

X
Stella's Hair
My daughter's hair has been styled to remind me of home:
one Friday night I prayed beside this head.
Whenever I look at my children I think there
are children whom the Germans would have killed.
My imagination has seen them starving and dead.

How can my daughter be protected from
such a weapon in the style of her hair?

XI
Encouraging Naomi
I encourage my youngest to think that she is important
I shall leave it to life to teach her humility
she looks English but was born a Jew
that she will suffer is certain

Though I can spare her nothing I can arm her
so that whatever happens cannot harm her
as much as what has happened has harmed me

XII

I Teach my Children

I teach my children independence all the time
I taught them to walk till they ran out of the house
I taught them to speak and they have made other friends
I teach my daughters to copy my hands with their hands
until they can do the work no longer mine
all the time I teach my children to say yes
to the beginning where their need for me ends

TOUCH (I)

A caress does more than appease
the hunger for touch:
practising the compassion of the flesh,
the body throws
—as music throws the dancer—
the mind into poses to please,
which mirror-poses answer.

TOUCH (II)

An accidental contact makes no claim.
A caress is different because it communicates choice.
Behind the touch which we are used to lies
a reservoir of bankrupt piracy.
Like ants at warfare signals issue from
unchallengeable familiarity.

MY MOTHER AT HOME

I

The colour in her bedroom was dark green,
an aid to contemplation. Someone said
that the aggressiveness of red would have induced
a calmer mood in her as compensation.

My mother liked to be locked up in sleep.

When I was innocent my mother was
a warm, white slug caught in a cabbage leaf,
blood-red hostility beneath her eyelids,
escaping effortlessly without moving
from all her sacred predators, to keep
the green and secret echo of her fire
safer than flesh from time's contamination.

In her deep sea she waited like a thief.

II

Beneath my fat and gentle mother was
the constant flapper as solid as her bones
screaming mercy into her sad face.
Everything she had salvaged to store away
corrupted and made clowns of her emotions
fiddling the booby-traps of everyday.

My mother waving in her rags of faith—
that was no challenge but her flag of truce.

MY FATHER AT HOME

I

Sometimes my mother stroked my father's hand
and he went out of the room, walked out of the house.
Three daughters said: 'This finger is for her,
this finger is for me, for me, for me,'
leaving the labourer his stubborn thumb.

My father loved four women faithlessly.

Beneath his daily uniform of life
squatted the fire-raiser at his trade,
scratching cold spoors to reveal
traps the savage urchin set.

My father screamed for untold help in sleep.

II

I sat upon my father's knee
like a lighthouse by the sea.

I escaped from where I sat
like rabbits when the corn is cut.

Like a battlefield I lay
when he got up and walked away.

III

The mermaid he had whistled from the rocks,
a sea-cow homesick for oblivion,
my mother sometimes wept in my father's arms.
I caught him flinching at the blubber-touch.
One might have thought three children tether enough.
But he adventured like one unaware
of life's eliminations and alarms.

IN THE NEW LIBERAL SYNAGOGUE.

I

How could Cain know what he had done the rabbi said
when he had never before seen this change
death came into the world with Abel dead

The listeners are exiled German Jews
sitting side by side each in his isolation
as a child I watched an angel choose
six million victims from this congregation
not to have died to have survived is strange

Let no one hesitate to mention to us
the killing of one human by another
the way to understanding passes through us

Cain did not know what he was doing to his brother

II

My neutral daughter is aware
that sheltered by my family
in God I am less close to her
than in the world's hostility

But can she see the mark we bear?

III

My daughter feels exempt and slightly bored
I have not taught her how to celebrate
now the traditions which I have ignored
challenge their echo in her to relate
her sturdy lifetime to the salvaged word

I think of children dying of starvation
six months I would have lived the records show
my feelings make a fence of all I know
between my daughter and this congregation

IV

I imagine my mother in any middle-aged woman
dressed in black warm and fat as she was when I was a
 child
my mind which can be compassionate to a German
has no pity for me and shows her about to be killed

V

The exiled choir sings its praise
in German Jewish melodies
we do not question God who made
men vulnerable and afraid
and others suffer more than us
nor in our father's house refuse
to rejoice that we are Jews

VI

Nothing this evening is for me what it seems
this synagogue is the symbol of another
my daughter is myself I am my mother
those around us have died in concentration camps
beyond this hall are other holy rooms
in which all the survivors worship together

AN EXAMINATION

The doctor demonstrated on my shins
that I was born into a time of famine
Germany nineteen twenty-three I said
not parentage but history determines
the substances from which our selves are made
beneath the jargon of my seven skins
my Jewish skeleton is branded German

ISRAEL NOTEBOOK 1966

I

Influenced by their own German childhood memories,
they told me not to burden my children with being Jews—
forgetting the wrecked lorries on the road to Jerusalem
commemorating the courage of those who died in them.

My half-Jewish children will grow up to make their choice.

In the *Yad Vashem* I heard an English child
asking: 'And he was going to be killed?'
intoning the statement like a ritual imposed
by every photograph of the holocaust.

'And they were going to be killed?' still asks the voice.

II

Anyone coming upon this grave without warning
might think some warrior king lies buried there
and that the names are of the battles he fought.
Six million dead need space only in thought.
If they could become birds they would fly clear
of this rock roof which will not admit the morning.

III

The salmon sun on camel ground
hatches ghetto beards of scrub
this is a concept more than land
to raise who were defeated up

IV

God's dereliction where he pottered Man,
green orchestration of Messianic dreams,
are the south and north of both exile and home,
where every year of the expectation of life
is represented by another nation—
all people whom the Germans would have killed.

V

Ancient Jerusalem is ruin-grey—
the ash of history raked to a crown;
oriental Jewish children play
within the range of rifles pointed down.

From desert stone, in legendary places,
an ancestry of pride is being built
by survivors with contaminated faces—
all people whom the Germans would have killed.

VI

That we come from the desert explains the Jew.
Where nothing obstructs the shadow of Man
or intervenes between eye and horizon
what can be imagined may be true.

A tyranny of concepts grew
in this petrified sea of pink and gold
where the world is what a life can hold.
The desert we come from explains the Jew:

Stunted, conditioned victims who,
yielding essence like a fruit,
danced in the presses of pursuit—
that we come from the desert explains the Jew.

VII

This is the country of the resurrection:
its people carry dead relatives in their eyes,
tend them for harvest in ghettos of remembrance,
hoard them against hunger where children are evergreen.

Behind the victims pilloried to pity
are granaries of healthy generations;
the whole dispersion irrigates this triumph
where history grows fresh interpretations.

JERUSALEM POEMS

I
The Wall

Jews in Jerusalem go to the Wailing Wall
to quell on stones a man-made desolation
here prayer has weathered scaffolding of thought
inexhaustibly to echo grace

Splinters of judgement in their ghetto eyes
their movements annotating dreams of slaves
for their rescue they haul from their heritage
with draughts of song a fragile jubilation

II
The Dome of the Rock

After the centuries-old donkey slums
the thronged mosaic of the market stalls—
the golden dome in space of sky and hills
blasts an exit for humility

What sprung in men to germinate this splendour
men whose descendants beg with retching eyes—
many-boned mortal hands of desert nomads
possessed by stones brought forth Jerusalem

The dome holds down the rock of sacrifice
cages the pulsing wings of aspiration
annihilates the difference between
life's enslavement and its celebration

III
Holy Places

Chasms in life we fence with ritual
to have faith means competing with others who have faith
in old Jerusalem the holy places
are hewn by legends out of history

Images blow the fuses of the eyes
where flesh imposed its features upon stone—
all we have is time and are comforted
to attest this cache of inconvertible alms

Whole aspirations are consumed like candles
we cancel ourselves to be appraised
buoyant impurities adhere to raise
five petrified redemptions to their trade

IV
Tombs

We write our scraps to God for crags in stones
nations will fight over till the Messiah comes—
trading for household the inimitable
the wings of life tangled in our lungs

Everywhere tombs subvert the dead from adventure
our ancestors whom excavations phrase
were desert turbulence—exhaled in whispers
where tourists waver and *Chassidim* pray

Extenuating passion we burn candles
to close horizons by a skin of smoke
grains of remembrance fasten on the membranes
as arteries we activate these walls

V
Landscape

All views are reminiscences of war
biblical and contemporary fights
are seasons in the landmarks hoisting time

The desert reared up to throw off such seed
and now it ruminates like basking camels

Where people have enslaved the soil it serves
worn raw in harness ploughing centuries—
mangy terraces quivering with growth

The burden generations have loaded on it
without letting it range makes one think it might
suddenly shake people out of its pelt and race
back into wilderness showering stones

VI
June War

1

They mourned the dead in the streets of Jerusalem
as if the plague of Auschwitz had come again
out of the ruins a radio reported
victories holocaust victories victory

There was only one dwelling damaged in the street
there was only one casualty, a middle-aged mother
they mourned her out of proportion to one death
because they were her children and had no other

A son's death reverses the current of time to a rage
air becomes blood and the parents suffocate briefly
they continue in glass tanks exhibited to pity

Every living gesture reminds of a life lost
every negation of life reminds of death

Their living bodies which could warm the dead
they have deserted to wake by the corpse

A dead son has to resurrect his parents
where memory touches animation grows
until they are reconstructed except for patches—
windows through which annihilation blows

A burnt-out tank remains—where are the dead
before this all reasons for war become obsolete
minds somewhere hold this event in parenthesis
the core of a cluster of obsolescences

A Jewish soldier sheltered an Arab boy
who will grow capable of manning a tank—
irrigate me cries the wilderness to the channel
flowing to feed the wheel that drives the war

The debris has been preserved as memorials
the weapons are sanctified by whom they have killed
and ambush all passing to donate some heartbeats
that they might rouse compassion like a child

VII

In the Military Cemetery

They lie together as they died in groups
my legendary boy who drowned at sea
Gabriel has his name engraved under water
'grieve faster' he called casting off all his unpossessed days

We put tokens on graves, be more dead to leave space for the
  living
underneath experience something stirs like roots—
visiting here what we pour as if into a mould
is the spare event, the vagrant empathy

Were they alive they would have nothing to waste
they would unravel time past to pass through the maze—
we hold on to their youth in our useless age
as fistfuls of seeds to lure them from their haste

VIII

Explosion

Today began days which began days ago
when some chose violence from all of life
broke daily bread domesticating death
and farmed destruction with the dung of hate

A bus full of children exploded in the desert
making a seismograph of every heart
setting alight a firework of fighters
the fuse of Auschwitz gaining on their birthright

Helicopters are flying over Jerusalem
tomorrow begins with the casualties of today
enmity is the closest relationship of all
more urgent than life, every death a regeneration

IX
David's Tower
Who are we to walk in Jerusalem
after two thousand years of contemplation
all the paraphernalia of our lives
domesticating the lava of a creed

Grey is the fortress made of singing stone
which was our drover through stress and fall
who have become mortar, tongue of the melody
grain for the threshing-floor in our father's house

As sling is to sword is David's to other towers
piping down exile, adjuring catastrophe
till the echo became people, flints in the shepherd's hand
and a column of ashes settled as seeds on the land

X
Auschwitz in Israel
There is a password changing Jews into
cells of one body under surgery
and mercy falls like agitated shadows—
we swarm to shelter in communication

From out of all the world's indifference
pushed or pulled, migrants flee to a stop
death has sunk wells in us but life makes fountains
transfusing residues into one nation

XI
Erev Shabbat

Jerusalem becomes one common household
we all keep pace with the setting of the sun—
holy is what increases through being shared
lives overlapping create reality

Emptying the week we open time
the space we offer determines the pitch it blows —
nightfall absorbs from us the everyday
joy is the surplus life we generate

XII
God in Jerusalem

Being in exile makes a Jew feel at home
orthodox people continue to wear ghetto clothes
transgressing centuries to be God's neighbours
pilot-lights burning and their lives ajar

Most of us others are exiled from God
the footprint on the obverse of the asphalt
the mines of desert where men prophesied
the membrances of the soil, the pulse in stone

The quarry leaping scorches memory
its call vibrates like heat-haze from high places
Jerusalem enters consciousness through the eyes
the convenant transluscent in its spaces

XIII

New Jerusalem

It was a concept not this modern city
which ghetto generations shored with prayer—
brooding in holy letters of lament
primordial shelter, ultimate ascent

Everyday living contradicts salvation
usage overrules the honey stone
everywhere people temporal and puny
dynamic bunting trade grace for event

An archway is this city awash with tradition—
in which we are humbled and exalted
a caravan from source to consecration
drummed through the centuries, never halted

I SET OUT FOR JERUSALEM

I set out for Jerusalem,
leaving my father and my mother,
when I sloughed off my childhood skin.
Before, when I was coined a Jew
by all the mints of Germany,
I set out for Jerusalem.
Before that, when my grandfather
with legends and with candlelight
forged for me a shield of pride.
When my infant senses met
reality instead of home,
I set out for Jerusalem.

I belong with those who kept
a Jerusalem of thought
as a refuge from the world,
guardians of splinters which
constitute our heritage.
Two thousand years of wilderness
from which the caretaker has swept
the excrements of history
are kindled to a radiance
in which motes of people dance—
pollen out of dust, to be
sustenance for prophecies.

Need to belong has made me come
to help rebuild Jerusalem,
where everyone is family—
all descendent from Abraham
and sharing one inheritance.

Where every step is taken by
one entering my father's house,
and every stone is laden with
the honey of remembrances,
my right hand is relearning to
renew me with community—
closer for containing me.

NIGHTFALL IN JERUSALEM

Purple, the light flows over the pallid stones
surrendering the pollen of the sun.
The desert drives its goats across the sky.

Messianic rock with people in its veins,
that has been crouching since the world began,
rises, each grain a fountain to the eye.

THE CHILDREN IN THE STREET

None of the children here ever walk on their own:
the scenes around them hand them through the streets,
their senses buckled into the armour of home.
Life kneels to its reflection in their faces.
None of the children are ever still, in response
to the sap of the city rising in their spring.

ENCOUNTERS

The ground is singing under our feet:
who were cast aside like stones have sprung up as harvest,
life rekindled by community.
The past ploughed under whispers as we meet:
you are my neighbour whose roots nourish me.

NAOMI IN JERUSALEM

I

One generation past the holocaust
my golden daughter matches Jerusalem:
all she expends herself on contributes to make her.

II

People, noises and events
are my daughter's elements
and the honey-coloured stones
dance about her in response.

A German girl came to my door,
saying she was the daughter of
someone I played with as a child.
I thought of how I was allowed
to use Margaret's garden swing:
that such a thing was event enough
forty years later to be recalled
implies the weight of the chains I wore.
I have lived with my memories for so long,
by now the poison has drained out.

My children walk in Jerusalem
engaged in life and unconcerned
that history makes use of them
to balance old iniquities.
They have no ghetto memories:
English country children who
belong to the Messianic age,
when the German sits down with the Jew
whom nothing now distinguishes
because his people has returned.

My children walk in Jerusalem
among the resurrected Jews
stronger collectively through them:
like jewels the crowd wears their eyes,
and future days bow down like sheaves.
All the graves of Europe have
closed before my children's gaze,
all the survivors have come through
a wilderness of grief to see
this Phoenix generation grow.

ON THE TERRACE

As sun reflected sometimes dazzles sight—
suddenly, in the midst of conversation
as I was sitting amongst friends at night
Jerusalem outlined in lights below—
my mind was dazzled by the thought of you
and I was glad, not out of calculation
because of what might come to me through you
but glad that you exist and that I know

NOTES TO CAROL
(for my grandson)

I

Babyhood to be complete
needs grandparents at head and feet;
six make a fence of family.
Michael's has been broken as
that of Michael's father was
by the hounds of history.

II

There is no such thing as the evil eye
and anyone may look at him;
but those who look at him don't see
the stopped earth of the fox of time.

III

Babies do not start from scratch.
Michael's caul told that I am
alien where he is at home:
before he grew his sense of sight
he crouched behind my eyes to watch
England receive me as a child.

IV

On a green island Michael grows
where villages bear legendary names
and moody seas dispute the rocky shore.
Before he learns to listen he will hear
the desert sighing in the summer rain.

MY TWO DAUGHTERS

I

My two daughters are the one fair, the one darker;
the colour of their hair is their badge of character.

II

The older one, my winter daughter, has
the quality of water under ice.
Like peasants from a lake, I draw
sustenance through the ice I thaw.

III

Stella harbours out of sight,
as bulbs do flowers, seeds of light;
she brings them out like ornaments.
Questing beast and quarry pause
to gaze through her forest eyes
at her firework of plants.

IV

Extracting colours out of mood
and patterns out of solitude,
Stella, like a sorceress,
compels adversities to bless.
An eagle urge beneath the skin
unpicks stars and thorns the shroud
of girlhood she is captive in.

V

As a well is to a fountain, Stella is to her sister,
who has no patience with passivity,
milks to exhilaration each fat day—
a Goldilocks who does not run away.

VI

All the adversities that attended her birth
were routed by a whisper of her worth.
Death left its hoof-mark on her scalp to turn
into good what comes to do her harm.

VII

Naomi, made to be
my ransom to history,
has fallen, to succour me,
far from her parent tree.
All of existence thrives
because she is alive.

VIII

My dandelion daughter moves
where faces turn as if to light,
I wish that she may always find
herself more loving than being loved,
and that what she seems at sight
does not belie the girl within.

STELLA GOING

I

My daughter has been leaving me all the time.
From the moment of birth I have been letting her go.
You cannot own daughters and all daughters grow
out of their father, their mother and their home.

Who am I to be discontent after seventeen years
that she is leaving me—can you call it alone,
when so much of me has turned Stella that I can
make her accept so much of myself as hers?

While life has been adding to Stella and Stella to me,
she has been going away from me all the time,
transferring to independence crumb by crumb
the mortar joining us as family.

II

Mothers are made out of the daughters they were.
I am pig-in-the-middle to my mother and Stella,
as if I were my mother and as if Stella were me.
I am the catalyst which those two share.

Stella is going from me as I went from my mother.
Continuity has blown its fuse in me,
imposing what was on what is going to be.
I am brand-marked 'mothers and daughters don't stay
  together'.

At every moment I remember how
I broke impatiently from the final embrace:

because of my failure as a daughter I face
what it meant for my mother to be my mother, now.

III
All conversations with
which I have tried to build
our relationship—
being mother and child—
into one holding good
throughout your adulthood
have been sabotaged by
my lack of experience of
being an adult daughter:
knowing my mother after
rejecting her where she stood,
which your going from me
now is a variant of.

IV
Don't look back at the anxious small woman who stands
with the reins you have slipped in her middle-aged hands,
she will cause you to stumble with a grey glance.
She will cast her blood as a river before you,
eject her womb as a wolf to devour you,
and dress her bones in your skin to dance.

Make for the gap in the hedge of horizon,
your parental pasture's become a prison—
time to begin your original fable.
Don't look back for the face behind the curtain,
it's the future about which you have to be certain.
Prove of what you're capable.

TONY

I

My younger son has tried to die:
swallowing sleeping pills to scrap
twenty-one years of growing up.
It makes no sense though he wrote why.

My gay and golden comforter
has come in from the world to lay
a stranger bearded beyond play
across the saddle of my care.

II

Tony is lying unconscious in hospital,
his dream of dying vomit in his mouth.
Doctors and nurses resurrect him with
first aid as if his hurt were physical.

III

Like honeysuckle Tony clung
when he was little and I was young.

He was fat and primed with life
when he got his first pocket knife,
trusted the arms of the sea
before he grew too big for mine
and learned to handle rod and line
before he knew his ABC.
He had a loyal passion for
toys that rose into the air.

He went through boyhood gathering
the cuckoo-spit of mothering.

IV

Tony put his feet up on the world's table,
believing it his birthright to be happy,
and round him grew a hedge of friends
sheltering him from life's demands.

V

Moony Tony longed to be
like a firework at night.
Moony Tony set alight
the gunpowder of reality.